Snow
White

Snow White

Written and illustrated by

Sally Gardner

Orion
Children's Books

Snow White first appeared in *A Book of Princesses*
first published in Great Britain in 1997
by Orion Children's Books
This edition first published in Great Britain in 2011
by Orion Children's Books
a division of the Orion Publishing Group Ltd
Orion House
5 Upper St Martin's Lane
London WC2H 9EA
An Hachette UK Company

1 3 5 7 9 10 8 6 4 2

ISBN 978 1 4440 0243 0

Printed in China

The Orion Publishing Group's policy is to use papers that are natural,
renewable and recyclable products made from wood grown in sustainable forests.
The logging and manufacturing processes are expected to conform
to the environmental regulations of the country of origin.

www.orionbooks.co.uk

For Shayane

 # Contents

Chapter One

One snowy day long ago, a queen
sat by her window sewing.
While she stitched, her thoughts went
to the baby she was going to have.

The queen pricked her finger on her
needle, and three drops of blood fell
on to the snow. She looked at the redness
of the blood, the whiteness of the snow,
and the blackness of the ebony window
frame and said, "I wish my baby's skin
to be as white as snow, her lips as red as
blood and her hair as black as ebony."

Soon after this the queen gave birth
to a beautiful little girl whom she named
Snow White. But happiness turned to
sorrow, for the young queen died.

The king was mad with grief.
He could not bring himself even
to look at his little daughter.

Snow White was taken away to
be brought up in another part of
the great palace, where her father
could not see her.

A year passed and the king married again. His new queen was very beautiful and very vain. Each day she would spend hours looking at herself in her magic mirror.

Then she would ask, "Mirror, Mirror on the wall, who is the fairest of us all?"

And the mirror
would answer,

"You, queen,
are the fairest
in the land."

The queen could not bear
to think that anyone was more
beautiful than she was.
What the mirror couldn't see
was the queen's heart, which
was ugly and cruel.

Chapter Two

Snow White grew up, long forgotten
by her father and hidden from her
stepmother the queen.

Snow White was very
beautiful. Her skin was as white
as snow, her lips as red as blood
and her hair as black as ebony.

Then one day the queen asked
the mirror her usual question.

It answered,
"You, queen,
may lovely be, it's true,
but Snow White
is far more beautiful
than you."

When the queen heard this she turned pale with rage and envy.

She called for her huntsman. "Take Snow White away and kill her. Bring me her heart so that I know she's really dead."

The huntsman took Snow White
to the edge of a dark forest where
bears lived and wolves howled at night,
but he could not bring himself to harm
this beautiful and gentle little girl.

"Run away from here, Snow White,"
said the huntsman. "Your stepmother
the queen wants you dead."

Snow White was so
frightened that she ran
straight into the forest.

The huntsman watched her go.
Then he killed a young deer
and placed its heart in a box
to give to the queen.

"I won't be lying when I say Snow White is dead," said the huntsman to himself. "For no one comes out of the dark forest alive."

Chapter Three

As Snow White went further into
the forest it grew darker and darker.

The trees tangled together and all
around her she saw the glinting eyes of
wild animals. Snow White was scared.
She fell and burst into tears.

But picking herself up,
she found to her surprise that
she was standing on a path which
led to the door of a little cottage.

"Maybe there's someone here
who can help me," she thought,
and she pushed open the door.

The lights went on and the fire began
to glow warmly. The strange thing was,
there was no one at home.

The cottage was neat and tidy.
In the middle of the room stood
a long table. On it were laid seven
little bowls and seven little glasses.

"Someone must live here," Snow White
thought. As if by magic all the bowls were
filled and wine poured into all the glasses.
Snow White was so hungry that she ate
some food and drank some wine.

Feeling very sleepy, she went
upstairs. There she found seven
little beds, neatly made.

She hoped that no one would mind
if she lay down on one of the beds and
had a rest. Soon she was fast asleep.

Chapter Four

This little cottage hidden away in the heart of the forest belonged to seven dwarves, who had lived there for as long as anyone could remember.

During the day they worked in
their diamond mine, and at night
they returned to their cottage.

Every night when they came home, the
lights would come on and the fire would
start to burn. Their bowls would be filled
with hot food and their glasses with wine.

Tonight, when they saw their little cottage, they froze. The lights were already lit.

"It's a burglar," said the first dwarf.

"Don't be silly," said the second.

They all went closer and pushed open the front door.

The food in the bowls was cold, and one bowl and one glass were empty.

"It must have been someone,"
said the third dwarf.

"Food doesn't get eaten by itself,"
said the fourth dwarf.

"Maybe it was a bear,"
said the fifth dwarf.

The sixth dwarf went upstairs
and came rushing down again.

"There's a girl asleep in my bed!"
he said.

"We'd better go and have a look,"
said the seventh.

In the morning Snow White woke
to find seven faces looking at her.

"Who are you?" they asked.

Snow White told them about
her wicked stepmother.

The seven dwarves had heard of
the cruel queen and they were
very worried.

"The queen is sure to find out that Snow White is still alive and come searching for her," said one dwarf.

"Yes!" said another. "She is only little, like us, and we must look after her."

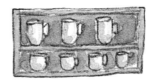

Chapter Five

All that day the seven dwarves
invented new things to keep
Snow White safe.

They fitted an alarm bell between
the cottage and the mine so that
Snow White could warn them
if she was in danger.

46

They built a pretend bear to growl if a stranger was about.

And they made some traps
in case the queen decided
to come this way.

The next day the seven dwarves
set off for the mine.

"Be careful, and don't let anyone into
the cottage," they told Snow White.

The queen believed Snow White
was dead, so she was happy.

Her magic mirror was silent.

Then one day, she asked,
"Mirror, Mirror on the wall,
who is the loveliest of us all?"

The mirror answered,

"You, queen,
may lovely be, it's true,
but the seven dwarves
hide one more
beautiful
than you."

When the queen heard this she was angry.
She decided she must kill Snow White
herself. She could trust no one else
to do it. She made two magic potions,
one of them poisonous, and the other
for her disguise.

She dipped a red apple in the poison.
Then she boiled the other magic potion
until only a teaspoon was left.

Staring into her magic mirror,
she drank…

The queen began to shrivel and shrink,
wrinkle and wither. Looking out at
her from the mirror was the face
of an ugly old woman.

The mirror turned black and broke
into a thousand pieces.

The queen put on a magic cloak that would make her as invisible as night.

She put the poisoned apple in
her basket and set off for the cottage
where the seven dwarves lived.

Chapter Six

Today Snow White was planning
to make an apple pie. She was a very
good cook and she loved to help
the seven dwarves.

It was growing cold and snow
had started to fall, when she heard the
pretend bear growl a warning.

Looking up, Snow White saw an
ugly old hag standing in the doorway.

"Hello, my dear," said the hag.
"I have the reddest of apples
in my basket! Would you like one?"

"This old lady doesn't look anything like
the queen," thought Snow White.
So she let the woman in.

"I pass this way once a year," said the old hag, "and I always leave some apples for the little men."

"That's very kind of you," said Snow White.

The old hag took the red apple from her
basket and held it out for Snow White.
"This one is just for you," she said.

"Oh, it's so red and shiny!"
said Snow White.

Snow White took one bite
and fell down dead.

The alarm bell rang in the mine.
At once the dwarves rushed towards
the cottage.

The old hag fled into the forest,
but her magic cloak got caught in
one of the traps and she was forced
to leave it behind.

Now the queen was invisible no longer. The dwarves chased after her as she climbed up the slippery mountainside.

A wolf howled and the queen missed her footing. She fell and was smashed to smithereens on the rocks below.

65

When the seven dwarves found
Snow White they were heartbroken.
They made a glass coffin,
with the words

HERE LIES SNOW WHITE,
A KING'S DAUGHTER

written on it.

Then they placed the glass coffin outside.
Ten years passed, and strange as it
may seem, Snow White kept growing,
and the tiny glass coffin grew with her.

One day a prince came riding by.
He had dreamt that his heart belonged to
a princess with skin as white as snow, lips
as red as blood and hair as black as ebony.
The moment he saw Snow White he
knew he had found her.

The dwarves did not want to part with
her, but they could see the prince
truly loved Snow White, so they decided
to give him her coffin.

The moment the coffin was moved, the piece of apple which had been stuck in her throat fell from her lips and Snow White woke up.

"Where am I?" she asked.

"You are safe with me,"
said the prince.
"I love you with all
my heart."

He knelt on the ground
and asked his beautiful
princess to marry him.

Snow White looked into the prince's
eyes and knew she loved him.

Snow White wanted the seven dwarves to be guests of honour at her wedding. Without them she would never have lived to meet her prince.

They all
went back to
the prince's
palace
together.

The wedding was magnificent, and it is true to say that Snow White and her prince lived happily ever after.

Look out for

Cinderella

Sleeping
Beauty

The Frog
Prince

The
Princess
and
the Pea